CHEAT CODES!

THE EMPOWERMENT MANUAL FOR THE WIFE

KRISTINA JOHNSON

CHEAT CODES!
The Empoweerment Manual for the Wife

Published by Kingdom Publishing, LLC
1350 Blair Drive, Suite F, Odenton, Maryland U.S.A.
https://mykingdompublishing.com

Printed in the U.S.A.

ISBN: 978-1-947741-91-1

Copyright ©2024 by Kristina Johnson

Unless otherwise indicated, all Scripture quotations are taken from the King James Version (KJV).

All rights reserved. No part of this book may be reproduced, stored in retrieval system, or transmitted in any form or by any means - electronic, mechanical, photocopy, recording, or otherwise - except for brief quotations in printed reviews, without the prior written permission of the author.

Cover design by Antonio Marlin Art
https://antoniomarlin.art

Dedication

This manual is dedicated to my endearing husband, Dr. Jasper Johnson. Baby, we made it!

I honor you; thank you for letting me love you. Thank you for never giving up on me. Thank you for learning and growing with me. Thank you for hanging in there through all the ups and downs. Thank you for your faithfulness, trustworthiness, genuineness, kindness, and kingship over our family.

It hasn't always been easy, and we still have trials, but nothing like what the father has brought us through. We've taught each other so much, and we have grown in leaps and bounds together. You're a man of few words to many, but to me, you're a man of many; when you speak, I listen. Honey, I encourage you to keep commanding the room. You will always have my support and undivided attention. I'll always be your biggest cheerleader, the one who makes the most noise and celebrates you for no reason, just because you're you!

I Love you!

Signed,
Your Sweets

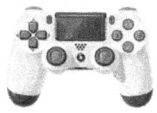

Preface

This manual isn't just a guide; it's a beacon, a lighthouse guiding you into the beautiful, complex world of marriage, particularly the role of a wife. It's a journey filled with intricate pieces, some of which we may unwittingly misplace, leading to complications we never intended. You might wonder, "Why should I listen to her advice on being a godly wife?" or "What gives her the right to write this guide?"

Well, this manual isn't a memoir of my personal struggles. Instead, it's a collection of lessons learned, a testament to resilience, and a celebration of love that has weathered storms. It's not about my story but the universal truths that can apply to all of you, regardless of the trials and tribulations you've faced as a wife and a mother over the years.

Despite the odds stacked against us, we managed to turn a marriage on the brink of divorce into a testament of enduring love. On the day the divorce proceedings were to be finalized, we chose to continue our journey as a married couple. This period of our lives, filled with sorrow and despair, unexpectedly transformed into something we could never have envisioned before we walked down the aisle.

Our bond, friendship, and love were not just restored but enhanced, stronger than ever. It wasn't a walk in the park. It took countless hours of work, introspection, tears, and arguments. It took years for us to heal, to learn, and to grow. Now, we can reflect on our past without being triggered, discuss our history, and learn from our mistakes.

CHEAT CODES!

So, back to the question of "what qualifies me?" I've done the work. As a military wife, a sports mom, a full-time worker, a student during all three of my pregnancies, a homemaker, and a full-time minister, I've juggled multiple roles. I've earned two degrees and my MSW, all while maintaining a healthy marriage and raising children. Like many of you, my story could go on, but I'll stop here. I hope you now understand that my qualifications extend beyond just being married to the father of my children for sixteen years at the time this manual was written. You don't need to know my life's tale, for this isn't a memoir of my past. I penned those words, and each poem is a fragment of my shattered, flawed, yet resilient existence. They paint a brief portrait of my life during a different era. But this guide? It hails from a place of completeness and exclusively delves into the wisdom of being a wife.

My journey through life's trials and tribulations, my struggle to conform to societal norms instead of discovering my true self, led to a labyrinth of confusion. My inability to communicate, understand, and see beyond his flaws paved the way for other thoughts to creep in, invading our home. Yet, amidst the chaos, we both still had miles to go. Was he always right? Absolutely not! Was I always right? Hardly. But we were both convinced of our correctness. This belief amplified every disagreement, making it loud, disruptive, and disrespectful, often culminating in me leaving the house only to return hours later.

It would be a glaring oversight not to acknowledge that our challenges weren't rooted in infidelity. Rest assured, he's been faithful, and yet, that doesn't lessen the ferocity of our struggles. I firmly believe that countless pairs have weathered storms far less severe and yet have failed to remain united. Furthermore, it's crucial for you to understand that if divine blessings have been bestowed upon your relationship, expect the forces of darkness to exploit any chink in your armor. Infidelity isn't the only threat; there are countless others. I'll delve deeper into this topic later in the guide.

THE EMPOWERMENT MANUAL FOR THE WIFE

Please be aware that this guide will contain words like "me," "you," and "I." This is because being a wife is a journey of self-reflection. You won't find my husband's story here, as it doesn't pertain to me. This journey is about me and about you. I'm thrilled that you've chosen to embark on this journey of self-discovery with me.

Join us on this enlightening journey! We're diving headfirst into the fascinating world of "submission" and stripping away its negative labels and cultural baggage. We're not just talking about the term "independent woman," but exploring what it truly means in the context of a loving union. We're shedding light on the importance of priorities in your daily life as a wife, and why prioritization is the key to maintaining balance.

We're going to challenge the conventional wisdom of phrases like, "I don't need a man." Instead, we're going to explore the characteristics of a good wife, such as being sensible, compassionate, caring, appreciative, warm, sensitive, encouraging, loving, trustworthy, humble, romantic, honest, creative, spiritually inclined, and so much more.

As you embark on this journey, remember this manual is not just a guide — it's a beacon of strength and empowerment. It's here to remind you of your power as a wife and daughter of the most high. So, as you turn the pages, let the words guide you through the challenging times, the times of uncertainty, and when you feel overwhelmed.

This manual is your secret weapon, your subtle hints to keep going, and to keep striving to be the best wife you never knew you could be. So, buckle up and let's dive in!

Picture this: from the outside, we women often envision marriage as a grand symphony of two souls harmoniously intertwined, brimming with unwavering love and deep affection. It's a storybook wedding, a spectacle of glitter and glamour, a day dedicated to showcasing your love and his devotion. You can step into the role of a princess; he's your knight in shining armor ready to sweep you off your feet and take you to a paradise that mirrors Eden's garden. This is a perfect union that emanates warmth, pure love, and the sweetness of marshmallows and lollipops. The yearning to be loved unconditionally by another, to have someone at your every call, someone who understands you better than you understand yourself. Someone who sees and hears you from a place of deep intimacy, a place of unspoken passion. This longing is the fuel that drives your desire to pledge your love in marriage.

This idyllic place of marital bliss, however, comes with certain expectations. These expectations are deeply rooted in our minds, a place that is accessible only to you and God. Not only are these expectations formed in our minds, but they also find their way into our hearts. The challenge arises when the opportunity presents itself, and that question we've dreamed of hearing since we were young girls finally comes. We seize the moment, expecting every wonderful thing to follow the words "Will you marry me"?

The moment the perfect man pops the defining question, what happens next? Well, we immediately call all our friends and loved ones; we share pictures of our ring and flood social media with posts of joy, hoping to garner likes, comments, and even stir some jealousy among those who may not be fond of us. Next, we set a date and embark on the journey of planning the wedding, assembling our bridal party, and ensuring that no loved one is left out. We find delight in choosing wedding dresses and coordinating color schemes, not to mention the countless hours spent on selecting the perfect centerpieces.

We then move on to try new DIY projects. We also begin scheduling dates and times for wedding venue showings, reviewing the menus, creating invites, and discussing the budget with our soon-to-be husband/spouse. We have lunch and dinner dates with the girls to discuss the ins-and-outs of the wedding day, including the honeymoon. Nevertheless, at this point, the bride-to-be has fallen head over heels for the wedding, and with every passing day, the desire to get to that day in time trumps anything else. Life has been cultivated by this very thing that, in a few short months, your last name will no longer be the same, and for at least one day, the spotlight will be on you!

The months turn into weeks, and those weeks turn into days, all leading up to the day considered the best day of your life. Riddled with nerves, you go headfirst into the festivities. First hair, second nails, and make-up, no care in the world; everyone is doing everything for you; your only job is to be pampered. Man, the anticipation is overwhelming, and your every sense is heightened. You can feel your heart beating through your chest as the moment gets closer and closer, and you can feel your breath get quicker and more rigid due to anxiety creeping in, in the form of reality.

Yes, reality peeks in, but only for a quick moment; some call it the wedding jitters, while I call it actualization. If only for a minute, something within you recognized the totality of the commitment getting ready to take place between two people who have no clue of what is hiding beyond the honeymoon. So, standing behind your bridal party, there you are, but at the beginning of life, you envisioned awaiting your time to shine, waiting for your time to glide down the aisle gracefully to meet your soon-to-be husband at the altar. It's finally your turn.

You smile nervously at the people gazing in awe at how beautiful you are. You're careful not to trip on that beautiful train while pretending your toes aren't turning blue from the pain your shoes are causing you. The defining moment has finally arrived. You are now standing beside the love of your life, the one who will provide everything your heart could ever desire. You both say your vows, kiss in front of your friends and loved ones, and move on to the reception. You have a blast with your family and friends at the reception. You and your husband enjoy the food, music, drinks, dancing, and laughter surrounding childhood memories and embarrassing stories. As you walk around the room shelling out hugs and kisses and receiving that same love back, you two are floating on cloud 9.

Hours later, the night ends, and your friends, family, and loved ones start leaving one by one, and you two are now interested in zipping away back to the honeymoon suite and/or wherever you have planned on ending your wedding evening. Everyone continues to party until the night comes to a complete end, and now you and your new husband open your eyes and enter the next day as man and wife. This bitter-sweet moment is welcomed with nervousness, joy, love, and great expectation for the days ahead, especially for the honeymoon.

You gather your thoughts and continue to enjoy one another; you get breakfast and bask in this unfamiliar and yet fantastic thing called love, and in the stillness of the moment, you two breathe in and breathe out and enjoy the rest of the day leading up to your honeymoon, if that's what was planned.

Many people, me included, don't think too far beyond the wedding or the honeymoon. Most times, our thought processes are limited to the here and now, and leading up to the wedding day, the adrenaline of expectation consumes us. Now, you may say, what about the people who seek marriage counseling before their union? Counseling before and during the marriage is always positive and, if possible, should be adhered to. Nevertheless, nothing can one hundred percent prepare you to have a healthy, loving, and endearing long-lasting marriage other than two people with the mental fortitude to want to make it work. Marriage is more than the wedding day, more than the honeymoon, and more than having an attractive mate. Marriage is work; marriage is not (50%) (50%), but both people must always be willing to give 100%.

Moreover, for the sake of this manual, I will be sure to focus on the "role" of the wife. I pray that as you read this manual, you will read

THE EMPOWERMENT MANUAL FOR THE WIFE

it with an open mind, and when you hear words like "submit" and "role," you will lean in for a clearer and healthier understanding. Welcome to Cheat Codes!

TABLE OF CONTENTS

Embracing the Concept of Submission
11

What Does Godly Submission Look Like?
13

What Do I Do When I Submit But...
15

Empowering the Wife or Wife-to-be
Cheat Code #1
Always Put Yahweh (God) First
19

Empowering the Wife or Wife-to-be
Cheat Code #2
Know Yourseelf, Your Identity Matters.
23

Empowering the Wife or Wife-to-be
Cheat Code #3
Never Uncover Your Husband
25

Empowering the Wife or Wife-to-be
Cheat Code #4
Make Yourself Available
27

> *Domestic Violence Support and*
> *the National Domestic Violence Hotline Information:*
> *www.hotline.org*
> *1 (800) 787-3224 or*
> *1 (877) 863-6338*

Empowering the Wife or Wife-to-be
Cheat Code #5
Self-care
31

Empowering the Wife or Wife-to-be
Cheat Code #6
Be Himble Even During Uncertainty
33

Empowering the Wife or Wife-to-be
Cheat Code #7
Be Gentle—Let Go of All That Masculine Energy
35

Empowering the Wife or Wife-to-be
Cheat Code #8
Understanding What "Do It Anyway" Means
39

Meet the Author
45

CHEAT CODES!

THE EMPOWERMENT MANUAL FOR THE WIFE

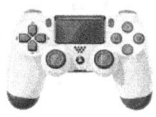

Embracing the Concept of Submission

When we hear the word "submission," it can stir up a whirlwind of emotions, especially for us women. It's a term that's often tainted with negativity, but let's take a moment to explore why that might be and how we can shift our perspective.

- We often confuse 'submission' with 'control'.
- We sometimes prefer the comfort of our familiar paths rather than venturing into the unknown.
- We try to merge spiritual principles with worldly beliefs, which can create a confusing cocktail.
- The fear of the unknown can be our biggest barrier.
- We often resist letting go of control, fearing it might make us feel powerless.
- Lastly, societal expectations and the fear of judgment can hold us back.

Now, let's break down the meanings of 'submit' and 'control' in the context of relationships.

Submit: It's about willingly giving up or yielding to a superior force or person's authority.

Control: This is when someone tries to dominate or take control over a partner in a harmful and self-centered way — that's abuse.

Understand that submitting to someone or something can be daunting is important. However, grasping the true essence of

CHEAT CODES!

'submit' is a key step towards embracing your role as a wife and being more mindful of your own journey, as well as those of others. This understanding is vital to navigating the path of submission in a healthy and respectful manner.

It's also important to acknowledge that submission in marriage can vary greatly depending on cultural and religious beliefs. For example, submitting to one's husband has deep cultural and religious significance in some societies. In some cases, what is seen as submission might just be misunderstanding or fear of the unknown. However, in other cases, what is perceived as ill will might just be a cultural or religious difference.

In this manual, we'll be focusing on the Christian perspective and approach to wifely submission.

THE EMPOWERMENT MANUAL FOR THE WIFE

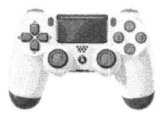

What Does Godly Submission Look Like?

As wives, we have been given the duty to submit.

Ephesians 5:22-24

Women, embrace a spirit of submission to your husbands, drawing a parallel to your relationship with the Lord. Remember, just as Christ is the head of the church, a husband is the head of his wife. This divine submission is not just about obeying commands, but about being committed, truthful, and trustworthy in your relationship. It's about honoring and uplifting your husband, recognizing that he is yours and you are his. But above all, it's about submitting to the Lord first, for it's only when we honor Him that we can truly honor our husbands. There will be times when you feel overwhelmed and tempted to seek fulfillment from your husband, but remember, the Lord comes first. This act of submission not only communicates your commitment to your husband but also affirms your devotion to the Lord.

1 Peter 3:1

In the same vein, wives, submit to your husbands. Even if they don't heed the word, your actions may speak louder than words. Your conduct can be a beacon that guides them towards the path of righteousness. But remember, this journey is not for the faint of heart. It requires embracing every emotion, good or bad, and understanding that being in the moment and saying "I do" comes with its own set of responsibilities. This manual focuses on the wife's perspective, but it's important to remember that responsibility lies on both shoulders.

CHEAT CODES!

1 Peter 3:1 also offers guidance on what to do when your husband doesn't see eye to eye with you. As wives, we're bound to have disagreements, notice inconsistencies, and point out things that irritate us. Despite all this, we are to draw our husbands closer to us with our character. This does not mean suppressing our feelings, concerns, or emotions. Instead, it means practicing humility even when we disagree, don't understand, and find it hard to yield to a man who may not fully grasp his role as a husband. Patience and self-reflection are key in this journey.

So, when you find yourself asking, *"What do I do when I submit, but..."* turn the page.

THE EMPOWERMENT MANUAL FOR THE WIFE

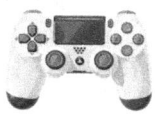

"What Do I Do When I Submit BUT..."

What do I do when I submit but...
- All things seem to be falling apart
- You don't feel heard
- You don't feel understood
- You feel as if you're doing everything you're supposed to, including submitting, but you are being mistreated.
- You may feel he isn't holding up his end of the bargain as a provider

No matter how you slice it, there's always a "but" that can't be ignored. It's crucial to remember that, even though these concerns might seem valid, it's imperative to express them with humility. Yes, this can be a tough task, and it might feel unfair at times. But remember, neither of you is flawless. You're both bound to make mistakes, and while you might be quick to point out his, he's probably doing the same, albeit in a less vocal way.

Next, let's talk about communication. It's easy to feel like a broken record as a wife, especially when you're the one always bringing up issues. But be careful not to turn into a nag. Give him time to process and respond, and repeat your points if necessary, particularly when it comes to important matters that need immediate attention.

Then, let's get creative. Incorporate your wants and needs into your daily routine. Think of fresh ways to catch his attention. I'm sure you've already thought of a few. Above all, don't assume he knows what you're thinking or feeling or what you need just because you're his wife.

CHEAT CODES!

Finally, keep your cool. Even though your "buts" are legit, you still need to submit. You're not submitting to the man he might become or his potential; you're submitting to the here-and-now and trusting in Yahweh (God) to guide your path.

This is what godly submission looks like compared to worldly submission. Worldly submission is defined as the act of giving in to the control or authority of another person. Submitting isn't just about cooking and cleaning, though these tasks are incredibly important and rewarding. Submitting is about serving your husband. For example, when I serve my husband his meal, I present it on a hard plate. I refuse to serve him on anything else unless we're at someone else's home. And I always serve him his plate before anyone else's because that's one way I show my love and appreciation for him. And just to be clear, neither our children nor I sit and watch him eat. I prepare everyone's plate, and he gets his first!

Now, let's move on. This is just one way I show my love and respect for my husband. There are many other ways you can honor the head of your household. It's about being intentional in how we respond to and interact with our husbands, especially during disagreements. Submitting means understanding that there's a role we must play. When we neglect this responsibility, we dishonor our households. Furthermore, since we have the power to shape the atmosphere in our homes through prayer, praise, and communication with Yahweh (God), we must use this power wisely to create an atmosphere of peace. Don't fall into the trap of thinking you are or need to be his peace. This mindset is flawed.

As wives, we won't always want to be his peace. We will have disagreements and arguments, and this is just the truth. It's not up to us to decide when or if these disagreements will occur. We feel like being his peace; it's not sustainable. The wise thing to do is give him to the one that created shalom (peace), the one who doesn't give and take it away, because even when we don't deserve it, He still gives it to us freely. I'm describing the unmerited peace, favor, and grace of Yahweh (God).

THE EMPOWERMENT MANUAL FOR THE WIFE

If your marriage is rocky, please seek outside help, including counseling/therapy. This manual is not taking place of therapy or medical diagnoses.

(Side note: no abuse of any kind is acceptable. Please seek help if this is the case). Any mistreatment that involves habitual infidelity, harm, or neglect should be reported if you are willing to do so.

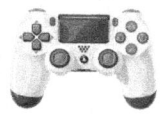

Cheat Code #1

Always Put Yahweh (God) First

Imagine this: you're standing at the starting line of a marathon, ready to embark on a journey of a lifetime. The race isn't just about speed or strength, but about endurance - who can keep going the longest. The Bible says, "The race is not given to the swift or to the strong, but to the one who endures to the end" (Ecclesiastes 9:1). This is the journey of marriage, and the one who endures, who puts (Yahweh) God first, will truly win.

As a wife, placing Yahweh (God) at the forefront of your life is of paramount importance. This relationship is distinct from the one you share with your husband. It's personal, unique to you. In this guide, we will explore what it means to put Yahweh first and how this impacts your role as a wife.

Remember when we talked about giving your husband to Yahweh? You might be wondering, "How do I do that"? The answer is simple—by putting God first! But what does that look like? It's different for everyone. When we set aside time to connect with our Father, we're opening the door to let Him into our daily lives — our children, our husbands, our careers, our friends, our families, and more. When we humble ourselves before Him, it becomes easier to humble ourselves in other situations, especially in our homes.

Now, let's talk about some key characteristics that every wife should embody for her own growth, sanity, and maturity and for the benefit of those she cares for, especially her husband. By practicing these traits, we can be healthy, independent women within our marriages while still submitting to our husbands.

CHEAT CODES!

1. <u>Sensible</u>: Make sensible choices, always considering practicality and reason.
2. <u>Compassion</u>: Learn to share in others' suffering and strive to restore. Be charitable, kind-hearted, sympathetic, tender, merciful, and forgiving.
3. <u>Appreciative</u>: Cultivate gratitude, give compliments, and do something your husband enjoys just because. Showing appreciation is crucial in a marriage.
4. <u>Honest</u>: Be truthful, even when it hurts. Honesty is vital to maintaining trust in your marriage.
5. <u>Encouraging</u>: Always support and affirm your husband. Encouragement can boost his confidence, especially when he's feeling low.
6. <u>Romantic</u>: Show love frequently, don't always wait for him to take the initiative, plan dates and outings, and shower him with gifts. Make him feel special.
7. <u>Creative</u>: Tap into your creativity, use your skills to solve problems, entertain, and create ideas that benefit your family.
8. <u>Trustworthy</u>: Be someone your husband can rely on, be dependable, steadfast, and honorable.
9. <u>Spiritually Inclined</u>: Maintain a relationship with Yahweh (God), read your word, pray, and worship daily. This is the most important characteristic to have.
10. <u>Educated</u>: Always stay curious, take courses, and keep your mind active.

When we put God first, we put our feelings, emotions, and motives on the back burner, giving us room to employ godly characteristics within our marriage, even when we don't feel like it. Remember, it's okay to make mistakes, to have disagreements, and to have moments of weakness. What's important is to understand that Yahweh has equipped us with the tools we need to get back up, try again, and continue on our journey.

So, be encouraged. The race isn't just about speed or strength but about endurance. Put Yahweh (God) first, and you'll find the strength to endure, love, and grow. You're not alone in this race; with God by your side, you'll cross the finish line.

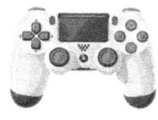

Cheat Code #2

Know Yourself, Your Identity Matters.

Hey there Sis,

Embark on the journey of self-discovery, understanding your inner self in depth. It's a voyage, a deep dive into your past and present, a process that might feel like a daunting expedition. But remember, it's all part of the journey to uncover your true identity.

If you're considering marriage, it's crucial to embark on this self-discovery journey before you say 'I do'. Marriage is a unique blend of two individuals, and it's important to understand that it can be complex. As a wife, you'll face challenges, learn new things, unlearn old habits, and constantly reflect on yourself. But remember, every confrontation in the journey of wifedom is an opportunity for self-growth.

Imagine you've mapped out your life's trajectory for the next five to ten years. You've done the groundwork; you know who you are, your identity, and everything else. Suddenly, a curveball hits — questions and tension arise during the dating phase, and you both overlook some crucial warning signs.

Fast forward to your marriage; your five-year plan has been disrupted, and you're questioning your identity. This is normal. When two people from different walks of life come together, it's a challenge to incorporate the complexity that marriage demands. This is why we, as wives, need to allow ourselves time and space to revisit our identity, not as independent women, but as women who desire independence as wives.

Being a wife doesn't mean sacrificing your identity or your desires. It doesn't mean your voice is silenced or your opinions are irrelevant. It doesn't mean you can't be successful or excel in different areas of your life. It doesn't mean you're less than or should be looked down upon. You can still find your niche, and you may have to put your desires aside occasionally, especially if you have children and are in the early stages of marriage. But remember, this is part of the journey.

As a wife, you nurture your children and your husband, ensuring everyone is well taken care of. Sometimes, we end up putting ourselves last or "when we find the time." The hard truth is that being a wife means laying your life down in a way that helps to understand the totality of your ministry.

Understanding who you are as a wife is different from knowing who you are as a person. As a person, you evolve, change, and shift over time. But as a wife, you need to adapt and learn to navigate this new identity. It's your responsibility to mold your personal identity into your identity as a wife. Keep God first, and you'll discover your true self.

As you embark on this journey, don't shy away from confronting the pain from your past. Don't be afraid to face your fears and insecurities. Being open with your husband about your insecurities is part of this journey. If you're not comfortable right away, that's okay. Take your time. Marriage isn't a race. We're all learning at our own pace.

Take a moment to breathe, remember that self-discovery takes time. No one becomes their true self overnight. It's a continuous learning process. So, embark on this journey of self-discovery, and embrace the challenges and opportunities that come your way.

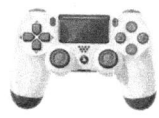

Cheat Code #3

Never Uncover Your Husband

In the sacred bond of matrimony, you two have melded into one entity, intertwined in every aspect of life. You share secrets that are meant for your eyes only, from past fumbles to present triumphs, from regrets to dreams of the future. This guide is succinct and to the point - don't reveal your husband! Let's delve into the term 'reveal.'

The term 'reveal' signifies the act of unveiling something concealed or unknown. It also implies the act of removing a veil to shed light on a matter (to spill the beans).

Your husband's journey to vulnerability might be a slow one, but when he does open up, it's crucial that you keep his confidence within the walls of your home. Being a sanctuary where he can be transparent with you is an honor, one that should never be breached. His vulnerabilities, his struggles, his fears - these are things that only you should know. If you find yourself sharing details about your marriage with a friend, make sure it's without casting aspersions on your husband.

Unveiling your husband not only puts him in the spotlight but also invites controversy, miscommunication, and potential conflict. And guess what? Unveiling him also exposes you. He is as vulnerable to spiritual disasters as he is to natural ones. So, keep him shielded, both naturally and spiritually, keep his secrets and conversations confidential, and keep your disagreements and arguments within the confines of your home. There will be times when you need to vent; if you have a trusted confidant to share your feelings with, who can offer a non-judgmental ear and hold you accountable, go ahead.

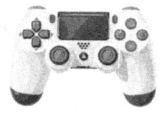

Cheat Code #4

Make Yourself Available

Get ready to unlock the power of cheat code number four! This secret weapon is not just a boon for your husband but also a gift for you. Let me unravel the reasons behind this, but first, let's break down the meaning of 'available'.

'Available' signifies being ready or prepared for use, obtainable, and present.

Now, let's dive into the meanings of 'present', 'suitable', and 'obtained'. Trust me, I'm about to take you on a fascinating journey. To be present means living in the moment, being fully engaged and focused on the here and now.

Think about the ways you can be there for your husband. I've left some space below for you to jot down three ways.

1. _____
2. _____
3. _____

To be suitable means executing appropriate behavior. Make sure your actions align with the man you've chosen to spend your life with. You're the perfect fit for him.

CHEAT CODES!

To be obtained means to be acquired or secured. You've been attained and have every right to feel secure. If insecurities creep up, don't hesitate to communicate them to your husband. Remember, he's learning just like you. The more grace you extend, the more he will reciprocate.

Make yourself available for communication, keeping in mind that not all communication is verbal. Sometimes, it can be tough to express your feelings; you might even struggle to find the right words due to your emotional ups and downs. But remember, it's normal and I'll be repeating this often.

Here are some additional nonverbal and verbal communication methods that can help you navigate through these challenging times. A quick disclaimer: you might not want to do all of these, especially if you're feeling unheard. However, remember that extending kindness can draw him closer to you. You'll have to push past your feelings and emotions to achieve this. Soon, you'll discover that there are some things you'll have to do anyway! So, it's best to accept this early on.

1. Pen a heartfelt letter or poem expressing your feelings.
2. Surprise him with unexpected displays of affection.
3. Plan romantic dates or fun game nights at home.
4. Send him thoughtful, encouraging texts throughout the day.
5. Pray with and for him.
6. Reiterate your desire to discuss your concerns openly.

Being present doesn't necessarily mean you're available. One way to ensure you're available is by being attentive. Try to understand your husband's physical and emotional needs. Ask him about his likes and show genuine interest in his responses. Remember, catering to his needs can enhance your marriage in the long run. Being a wife is a labor of love that comes with its rewards. Hear me when I say it's work, but harmony will prevail as long as you both are committed to acknowledging this and working towards a shared understanding within your marriage.

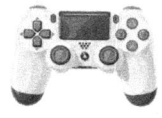

Cheat Code #5

Self-Care

Hey there! It's crucial to remember that you can't pour from an empty cup. So, start by taking care of yourself first. Self-care isn't just about getting your hair and nails done, although that's a nice treat when you can afford it. It's about nurturing your mind, body, and soul in ways that are sustainable and meaningful. Here are some ideas to help you incorporate self-care into your daily, weekly, and monthly routines.

First off, let's talk about money. Some might argue that your husband shouldn't always foot the bill for your beauty treatments. If you're not working, this may not apply. But if you're not working and still expect your husband to cover your hair and nails every few weeks while juggling the bills and keeping a roof over your head, that might be a bit self-centered. So, consider buying a manicure kit and letting him treat you when he can. If you're working, it's perfectly fine to use your earnings for these treats.

Remember, there's no need to stress your partner out about your hair and nails, especially if you have kids and he's doing his best to provide. Trust me, he already finds you incredibly beautiful. So, let's focus on the bigger picture. I've learned in my marriage that a genuine man loves to pamper his wife, and this affection can grow over time. Give him some space, but don't pressure him. Here are a few more self-care tips:

1. Digital Detox: Try to limit your time on social media, especially when you're feeling emotionally drained. It's

important to avoid comparing yourself to others when you're not feeling your best.
2. Mindful Breathing: Take a moment to focus on your breath and notice how your body feels. If you're stressed, you might find your shoulders creeping up towards your ears. This is a signal to relax and let go of tension.
3. Saying No: Learn to say no and prioritize your tasks. Use a planner or a calendar to keep track of your commitments. Don't overcommit yourself, and remember, your home is your priority.
4. Prayer and Meditation: Make time for prayer and meditation. This is where you draw your inner strength. It's essential to nurture your spiritual self, and it's beneficial to learn how to alternate between prayer and meditation.
5. Seek Professional Guidance: Consider seeking counseling or therapy from a qualified professional. Therapy isn't just for dealing with past issues but can also provide support, guidance, and leadership. A proactive approach can help create a more balanced home environment.

Now, let's brainstorm some more ways to pamper yourself. For example, you could incorporate reading into your routine. Use the space below to list your ideas.

a.

b.

c.

Once you've identified some self-care activities, the next step is to prioritize them. Place yourself at the top of your to-do list. This isn't selfish. When you prioritize your needs, you can then be a better partner and parent for your family.

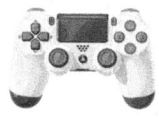

Cheat Code #6

Be Humble Even During Uncertainty

Imagine the bedrock of this guide as humility. Yes, you heard it right! It's not just a foundation, but the very essence that shapes this manual. Now, let's dive into the paradox of humility. It's a double-edged sword, with its perks and pitfalls unfolding in different scenarios. Yet, one thing remains unchanged - a humble wife is a beacon of praise.

Peter 5:5 echoes, "Clothe yourselves, all of you, with humility towards one another, for God opposes the proud but gives grace to the humble."

Ephesians 4:2 whispers, "With all humility and gentleness, with patience bearing with one another in love."

Humility is the secret sauce that infuses grace into our relationships. It's about extending kindness even when our spouse might not be on our wavelength. It's about maintaining our humility in the face of uncertainty. It's about understanding that humility can be a game-changer for our marriages. The trouble begins when the tug-of-war ensues, with neither party wanting to back down; neither wanting to be the bigger person. Both parties are hell-bent on saving face, even if it spirals into disrespect.

Picture this - both of you are locked in a verbal duel, with each trying to outdo the other. It's a common scenario, and I'm here to remind you that you have the power to diffuse these situations. You may not always choose to, and that's okay. But remember, being humble is a two-way street. As a wife, it's like a garment you wear.

Before we part ways, I want to share a secret with you. Before you can wear the garment of humility as a wife, you must first humble yourself before God. Many, including myself, didn't truly understand humility until our marriages were put to the test. I didn't know how to humble myself correctly because I hadn't fully submitted myself to the Father. Humbling yourself before the Lord teaches us how to embody a Christ-like spirit. But let's be clear, this doesn't make us perfect, nor does it guarantee that we will always be the bigger person. After all, we're human, and we're not always going to turn the other cheek. So, be gentle with yourself. Give yourself time, and remember, it's okay to stumble. Because here's the truth—marriage is a journey, not a destination!

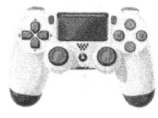

Cheat Code #7

Be Gentle—Let Go of All That Masculine Energy

From an early age, I discovered a deep-seated desire to take charge. I felt no one could surpass my capabilities. My journey as a military serviceman for a significant period, coupled with the unique challenges of being a black woman in America, further solidified this belief. It's unfortunate, but black and brown women are often perceived as overbearing, loud, and disrespectful. Yet, this is not always the case. For many of us, our vocal and energetic demeanor is a reflection of our culture, especially when expressing our emotions.

As I delved deeper into the topic of toxic masculinity and its implications on femininity, I was compelled to confront the role of trauma in shaping our identities. We are often conditioned to believe false narratives about ourselves and others. This conditioning, coupled with the residual effects of 400 years of oppression, leads to internalized racism and complacency among black people.

The black man and the black woman have historically been pitted against each other, often due to external influences. This has contributed to the breakdown of the black family and the consequent impact on our emotional regulation, societal interactions, and overall behavior.

As we age, the conditioning we received as children persists into adulthood, leaving little room for self-awareness. This is especially true when it comes to how we react to situations.

CHEAT CODES!

Reflecting on our roles in marriage is crucial for personal growth and the health of our relationships. Toxic masculinity and the need for independence can negatively impact our unions. This term, often associated with destructive male behavior, can also apply to harmful, misguided behavior from women.

Before we proceed, I want to emphasize that if this discussion triggers any discomfort, that's a positive sign. It means you're engaging with the material.

Now, let's talk about the role of the wife. There's a certain way we should conduct ourselves, but it's important to remember that no wife gets it right all the time. The key is to strive for grace, both within and outside the home.

One crucial aspect of self-improvement is the willingness to unlearn harmful habits and behaviors. This requires introspection and the courage to confront our flaws.

Being a wife requires relinquishing some control, a challenging task, but necessary if you're to submit to an honest man. Submission isn't about abandoning your individuality or surrendering your identity. Instead, it's about learning to collaborate with your partner to foster harmony within your home and marriage.

If you're married and reading this, you've already chosen the man you've decided to spend the rest of your life with. If you're single and reading this, take note of the advice I'm about to share.

People often advise against performing wifely duties for men you're not married to. I agree with this advice to an extent. If you're dating, you should display certain qualities that make you a potential wife. However, I don't advocate for wifely submission while courting. Your attitude and willingness to nurture should be evident, especially after you've both agreed to pursue a marriage.

THE EMPOWERMENT MANUAL FOR THE WIFE

Letting go of masculine energy creates space for your husband to thrive in his natural environment. I'm aware that women tend to be defensive, suspicious, and cautious. Such emotions can be perceived as aggressive or belligerent. However, these behaviors are often the result of unhealed wounds and the influence of our environment.

Let's also discuss the importance of attraction. Every woman wants to be attractive to her husband, right? This attraction should extend beyond physical appeal and into emotional and spiritual realms. When you allow your femininity to shine naturally, it encourages your husband to go above and beyond.

Being free of masculine energy also means you don't have to worry about masculine issues. Your husband has it covered. He may take some time to find balance, so be his helpmate and extend your support where and when you can.

Remember, some men aren't taught to be...
And women have to learn to be...

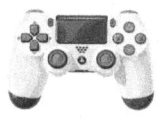

Cheat Code #8

Understanding What "Do It Anyway" Means

As we draw this guide to a close, let's kickstart a conversation about the meaning of "do it anyway." You know, I get it—you're weary from constantly being the bigger person. You're fed up, ready to throw punches, but hang on a minute! Refocus, keep your hands off him, and keep your thoughts pure. Remember, I never promised you a walk in the park. In fact, being a wife is something you can never truly prepare for, making it one of the most challenging yet rewarding roles we can ever undertake. So even when you're feeling a bit low, "do it anyway."

"Do it anyway" when you're not in the mood to cook or set his plate because of a tiff or disagreement. When you're not in the mood to pick up that worn-out sweatshirt he left lying around, just hang it up! You'll have those moments when you talk until you're blue in the face, and he just doesn't get it; that's just the reality. However, as you learn more about your husband, you'll start to understand his ways, and your approach will change. Now, I'm not suggesting you should clean up after him like a child; that's not what I mean. I'm talking about those little things that bug you like when he leaves water on the floor after a shower or a towel on the bed? These things can be annoying, especially if you prefer a tidy, organized home.

You might already be nodding your head if you're married. Let's change our approach and "do it anyway." Sometimes we just have to do what we have to do, whether we agree or not; it's just the way it is. Would you rather stress yourself out or handle it? There will be days when he'll drive you up the wall, and "do it anyway" might be the last thing on your mind. If and when that happens, take your time, breathe, and let no one else do it. It's times like these when neither of you should do anything and just breathe. You'll sometimes be overwhelmed; you'll drop everything and think, forget this; you're past the sunshine and lollipop phase of your marriage, and now it's time to put in work. Sometimes you'll feel like a mother to your husband. That is because he may be treating you as such. This can happen subconsciously and sometimes consciously in his mind and can result from many things, regardless of the reason,

There may be a time when you'll have to mother your husband. Don't let the stigma of this narrative make you bitter. One might ask, "What does that look like?" Well, it can look like many different things. For example, it may look like you running his bath water when he comes home from work, and after he takes a bath, maybe you rub him down with oil or maybe you caress his head and lay his head in your lap or maybe you massage his feet or give him a back rub or back massage.

Perhaps, mothering your husband looks like you looking past some of the things we talked about earlier, those the things that may be a bit frustrating or annoying to you. Maybe it's you just taking him by the hand and telling him how much he means to you or asking him what he would like to do. Maybe it's just you understanding that your husband has yet to be taught how to do what you require of him to meet your expectations. So, as a result, you supersede what he is knowledgeable of. Please remember that he's doing what he knows how to do, just like we, as wives do. As wives, we do what we know, and we often have to learn on the job, but either way, we desire grace. In that same way, extend an olive branch to your husband extend grace until things turn around for the better. If he makes a mistake, don't emasculate him, but bandage him, pick him up, and encourage him to fight another day.

When it comes to managing finances, your husband may not be the best provider; maybe you didn't know this before marriage. Either way, in marriage, we have to work with what we both provide for each other; perhaps your strong suit is finances. We as women often get so caught up in the men being the providers, and guess what? Yes, that's biblical and correct. However, being a provider doesn't limit him to monetary gain; that's just one aspect. Although that's significant, it is still only one aspect. There are some marriages where wives earn more money than their husbands, and that's fine, while in some other marriages, the wife handles the finances. Whatever works for you in your home, let it work for you.

If finances are an issue, seek financial assistance through a financial advisor because mishandled finances can cause significant problems within your marriage. If work ethic or lack thereof is an issue, seek help outside of your marriage, such as therapy and/or counseling, to help you both work through this. Have these hard conversations because it is essential to communicate the importance of being on one accord about finances. Remember, although you may be called to mother him for a time, he is not a child.

This guide demands a lot from you as a wife and as an all-around person. I need you to know that there is no greater feeling when everything is reciprocated. Your man may not know how to pamper you, but you can teach him. He may not know your favorite color; tell him. He may not know that you like to go on walks; just take him with you. You'll have to teach him your love language and be responsible for learning his. This is what a God-fearing marriage looks and feels like through the lens of a woman willing to be selfless. So, as you walk this path, keep your business to yourself and find a support system in other wives (who aren't bitter). This support system is not a group of women who gather to talk about all the bad stuff, but to uplift and pray because they already understand the things that need not be said.

Lastly, take time for yourself, whatever that looks like for you. Please don't be so hard on yourself. Remember, you said, "Yes." So, there was a time when he was enough!

Resources

National Domestic Violence Hotline
PO Box 90249
Austin, Texas 78709
Administrative Line: (737) 225-3150

Wifely Approach LLC
Kristina Johnson MSW, LMSW
Owner, Founder, and CEO
https://www.thewifelyapproach.com/

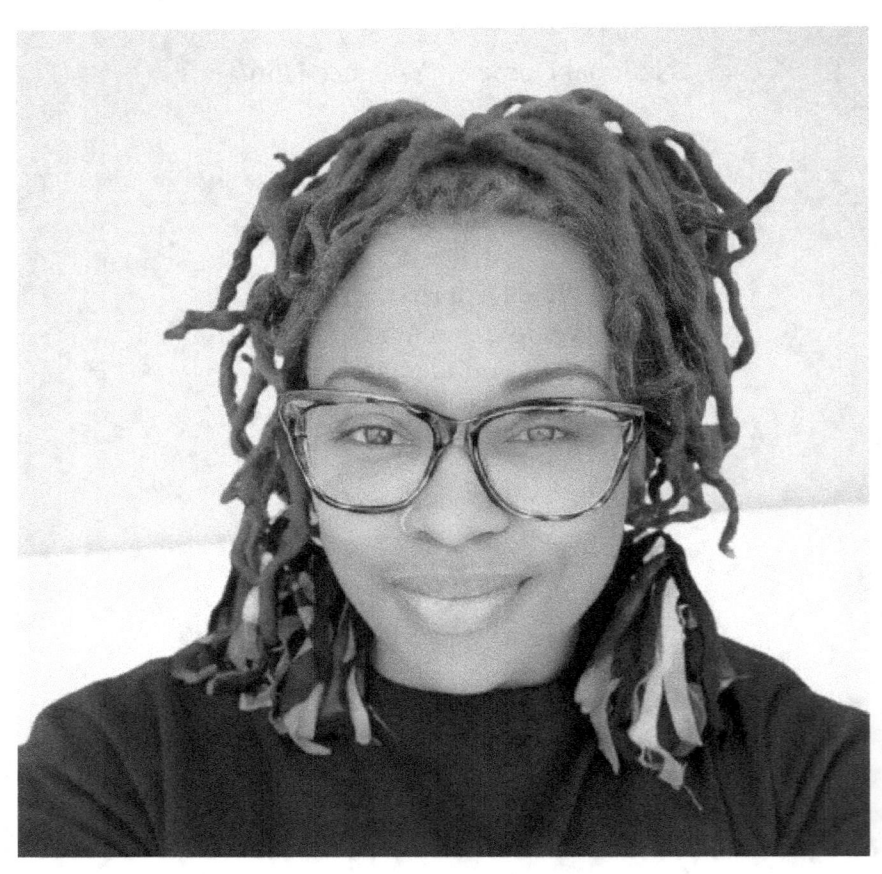

KRISTINA JOHNSON, MSW

Meet the Author
Kristina Johnson, MSW

Meet Kristina Johnson, MSW, a dynamic two-time author, CEO, and proud owner of The Wifely Approach, LLC. She's not just a businesswoman, but she's also a devoted wife and mother of three. Kristina has instilled her wisdom into eight essential "codes" that are designed to empower women to navigate their marriages successfully.

Imagine a self-help guide that feels more like a friend's advice filled with practical tips and strategies to help you weather the emotional rollercoaster that is marriage. That's exactly what Kristina's manual offers. It's not just a book, it's a journey—a journey of self-discovery and growth that can help you turn the challenges of marriage into opportunities for personal and relational growth.

Kristina's "codes" are not just theoretical concepts; they're born out of her personal experiences. She's been there, navigating the highs and lows of marriage, and these codes are her hard-earned wisdom. She learned them the hard way, and she wants to spare you that journey.

But let's face it, we all walk our own paths, and our stories are unique. The complexity of being a wife is a shared experience, but the details of our journeys vary. That's why Kristina's manual is such a valuable resource. It's not about reaching a destination, but about embracing the journey—filled with unexpected twists, turns, and the thrill of discovery.

So, are you ready to open your heart and mind to the reality that saying 'yes' is just the beginning? Are you prepared to do the work? Kristina's manual is here to guide you on this exciting journey of being a wife. Let's embark on this expedition together.